CHAOS
AND THE
AFTERMATH

**COLLETTE
SCANDRETT**

Chaos and the Aftermath
Copyright @ 2021 by Little Publishing, LLC

All rights reserved. No portion of this book may be reproduced, stored in a retrieval system, or transmitted by any means electronic, mechanical, photocopy recording, scanning, or other except brief quotations without prior written permission of the publisher, except in case of brief quotations embodied in critical reviews and certain other noncommerical uses permitted by copyright law.

For permission requests, write to the publisher, addressed "Attention Permissions Coordinator," at aalittle08@gmail.com

Published By: Little Publishing, LLC
Little Publishing, LLC
aalittle08@gmail.com

Ordering Information:
Quantity Sales: Special discounts are available on quantity purchases by corporations, associations, and nonprofits. For details, contact the publisher at the address above.

ISBN: 978-0-578-33360-1

PRINTED AND BOUND IN THE UNITED STATES OF AMERICA

TABLE OF CONTENTS

Drowning in Doubt 1	Reminders 50
Real Worth 3	Torn World 52
Your Kingdom 5	Nightmares 53
Everyday 7	Blurry Picture 54
Newfound Fears 8	Mistaken Strength 55
Sadist Naïvete 10	Never Mine 57
Reality of Fate 11	Doubts 59
My Art 13	Delusional Love 61
Benefits Unseen 15	Promise 63
Perfect Soul 17	My Apology 64
My Prison 19	Trust 66
Outgrown Life 21	The Nation I Love 67
Pains of Tomorrow 22	Real Love 69
Unwanted Tomorrow 24	Future Wife 71
Always Care 25	The River 73
Desolate Road 27	Raw Emotions 74
Lies Believed 28	Judgment 76
Entitled 29	Hidden Emptiness 77
Calmer Days 31	Descending Darkness 79
Harvest Colors 33	Forgotten Face 80
Nightly Show 35	True Enemy 82
Unknown War 36	Will to Live 84
Respect 38	State of Life 86
Waiting in Vain 40	Without Response 87
True Fortitude 42	Mirrored Pasts 89
Still the Masters 44	Your Sunlight 91
Hidden Hatred 46	My Mermaid 92
Only 12 48	

DROWNING IN DOUBT

Why do I feel jealous
When they seem to get on track?
After all I did to help them
I no longer have their back
If I focused on myself
Like I had focused on them
I might have gained some of the things
I have wanted for years

It's like I purposely divert myself
From having happiness
Like all the pain and misery
Is all I know to live
Never wanting to focus
And find my own way out
Helping others find the way
While drowning in the doubt
The doubt of who I'm supposed to be
Or what I'm supposed to do
The doubt of many failed attempts
Of the caring heart subdued

continued…

One day I hope that the pain
Will no longer be my home
That there will be a way
To finally let go
But until that day
I will circle around again,
Continuing to give while they take
Until I have no more to give
And there is nothing left to take

REAL WORTH

Agreed to live this life,
Knowing how it came
The feelings grew much deeper,
Hoping you would feel the same
But I guess it was too much
Which I couldn't see back then

So engulfed in all my feelings
All that I could see was pain
The pain of being scorned
Or being left alone
The pain of being nothing deep
When I thought that we had grown
Maybe it was me who grew
Out of my childish ways
No longer fearing the serious
Or the strings with which it came

I am sorry that I blamed you
For being who you always were
You never tried to hide these things

continued…

Which in itself is rare
You taught me I could love
Even if it's just myself
You taught me how to recover
No matter how bad it hurts

I will love you forever
Not because you were my first
But because you helped me discover
What my love is really worth

YOUR KINGDOM

Memories of the awful days
Being shunned for being me
Treated me like an imposter
So many following her lead

I never wanted to infiltrate
The circle you clearly defined
Fine with being on the outskirts
And waiting for the time
The time when your reign was over
And your kingdom would disappear
When your trusted court would leave you
And reality would reappear

The real world will not bow to you
Or hang on your every word
The magic you held over so many
Would disappear with one word
This will probably be your highest point
In the kingdom you built for yourself
As your insecurities start to show

continued...

I can see why you surrounded yourself

With minions that could
only see what you wanted

Not the sad and pitiful truth

The person you buried deep inside

And wasn't seen too often

That you were sincere and vulnerable

And hiding from herself

That you could accomplish many things

And thrive in the real world

Thankfully those days have ended

And I no longer have to care

The real world has taken over

And your kingdom has disappeared

EVERYDAY

As the days pass,
And the pain grows deep
The light continues to dim
The memories continually flood
Through the broken dam
My mind continually built

Now so many thoughts
That had once faded away
Are finding their way in
With each passing day
My heart grows numb to everything
That doesn't pertain to her
The day that I never wanted
Now becomes my everyday

I hope she knew I loved her
I hope she knew I cared
That I would give away my life
For her to still be here
My mom was all I ever had
And now I'm down to nothing
The only relief in sight
Is joining her in the hereafter

NEWFOUND FEARS

Fearing what's to come
But not knowing what it is
Seeing all the devastation
Inciting all our fears

How do we stop something
We know nothing about?
With a presence so powerful
It's disturbed our whole life

Just to go to the store
Takes a newly found courage
Is it worth the risk?
Or can I just do without it?
Now things are reopening
But does that mean it's safe?
Or are they as stir crazy as me
Having to stay in the same place

Would you risk my safety
For your material gain?
Or can I trust the worst is gone
And I can safely move about again?
I think I'll wait and see how it goes
For the first ones going out
Hopefully, it will turn out well
And allay any further doubt

I want this to end soon
As the fear is driving me insane
Your impression will always linger
And I will always remember your name

SADIST NAÏVETE

Why do I continue
To keep going back
Why am I convinced that pain
Is all that I can have?

You treat me like your once bought slave
Used for sex and money and more
Treat me like I am nothing to you
As you search for your next whore
I come back to the pain
Like I'm some sort of sadist naïve
Trapped inside your mental game
Like I don't know how to leave

I guess I hope you find your next,
So you can toss me to the side
More than you've already done
On this twisted morbid ride

REALITY OF FATE

The more time passes
The more the fear sets in
Mulling over the very thing
I've been dreading for years

No longer just a diagnosis
But now a part of life
Now understanding the many warnings
So often pushed to the side

I am too young for this
These things don't pertain to me
Save your lengthy lectures
For someone actually in need

I'm healthy and athletic
As I have always been
I don't need the looks of sympathy
But I'll make sure to tell you when
When I need your doctoring
Or when I need your help

continued…

The never-ending barrage of pills
You can surely keep to yourself

Right now, I'm calm and happy
In my created delusional space
Where I hope to spend so many years
Avoiding my eventual fate

I will stay here until I'm dragged out
By the reality of fate
And can no longer avoid the struggle
Which is all that will remain

MY ART

The beauty that most aren't able to see
As they can't see past the surface
The intertwining of colors and dreams
Splashed beneath the surface

The way that some choose to express
Misinterpreted by most
The art that lasts the test of time
With each familiar stroke

I think of all the many designs
That reflect who I feel I am
The edicts and illustrations
That will be perceived by others

Those who look on in dismay
At something they can't understand
Or those that feel they know my pain
From glimpses of who I am

continued...

The art that they are able to relish
Or for some more so tolerate
Is really just a way for me
To remember what I have endured
And remember what feels like endless pain
Only shadows contrasted to the light that remains

BENEFITS UNSEEN

You built in me a sense of faith
And belief in something unseen
The faith to trust before I know
And think things are as they seem

Trying to see the best in people
And help others when I can
Putting myself in tough situations
Just trying to lend a hand

You said knowing I helped would be my reward
As many will not show gratitude
That some may be too proud to ask
Or even give off an attitude

I can't ignore their plights for help
Even when they are not said
Because saying no always haunts me
With their pictures of despair in my head

continued…

I wish you had not taught me these things
As so often, people take advantage
I hope one day to rid myself
Of this seemingly perpetual burden
I don't intend to stop helping
Maybe just not everyone I see
Because when I get in a bind
There is no one there to help me

I know I shouldn't complain
If I have the ability to help
But I guess sometimes I just wonder
When the benefit will be for me

PERFECT SOUL

When will I get to meet you?
The one I'm meant to love
The one I've searched for my whole life
That never-ending love

I thought for a while I had
Or maybe I just hoped
Or maybe I just became complacent
In just playing a role

I think of what you will look like
How beautiful you will be
With the perfect personality
That will bring me to my knees
Take me back to praying
Which I lost so long ago
To express my complete appreciation
For creating such a perfect soul

continued...

I hear your voice in my head
As I plan our life for the future
The house
The land
The kids
And the time to get lost in them

I plan to work hard now,
So all can be enjoyed
With this person I've dreamt of for so long
This beautiful and incredible soul

MY PRISON

Another night I can't remember
As it all remains a haze
Giving in to the very thought
That I can't remember days

Days that may be filled with joy
Or unforgivable actions
Nights that I can't seem to access
Maybe for my own satisfaction

I'm not sure why I indulge anymore
As the worst memories still remain
Thinking it the perfect way out
But it no longer erases the pain

The pain I've felt for so many years
That it seems a daily occurrence
The guilt that I can't seem to shake
No matter the way I try

continued…

The memories that invade my thoughts
When I happen to let my guard down
All will never be forgiven
As I can never forgive myself
The memories of who I used to be
In my unforgiving past
The punishment befitting the crime
With its everlasting effect

Time the only pardon available
For this prison within myself
The time when all else fades away
And life is no longer lived
Will provide me with the final forgiveness
That I don't deserve to live

OUTGROWN LIFE

Just another day
For me to hate being me
Just another time
For my sensitivity to be seen

As the misery sets in
So does the sadness
Now this deep darkness
Has taken over my gladness

No longer joyful
Or happy with life
Where there once was a smile
Now there is only strife

I have now outgrown things
Once enjoyed in my youth
I feel like I've outgrown life
Is my real truth

But maybe one day the light will reappear
Although it is doubted that this day is near
But until that day, I will dwell in the dark
Because I've been hurt deep to my heart

PAINS OF TOMORROW

Feelings rushing over me
Pulling me in every way
Different feelings coming through
With every passing day

Feelings of despair
Making me pull out my hair
Feelings of sadness
Overcoming all gladness

Feelings of regret
For things that should've been set
Feelings of hate
For the person I've made

Feelings of dumbness
Overcome by a numbness
A numbness for being stupid enough to believe
That anything could ever go right for me

But most of all,

Even though it's last

I probably should've learned from my past

A feeling of sorrow

When I think of tomorrow

For it only holds pain

Like every other tomorrow

UNWANTED TOMORROW

Tomorrow is just another day
For me to hate and regret the day
The day that I was born
The day that I left home
The day I was conceived
The day that I became me

I wish once again
I could go back to that day
When she made that decision
And tell her it's okay

Okay for her to let me go
To tell the doctor not to hold on
To save me from the pain and gripes
To save me from this thing we call life

It was not worth the pain it brought
And it is no longer sought
Now I can't let it go
Because my life has such a hold

A hold into yours as a part of you
And for that very reason
I'm trying to make it through

ALWAYS CARE

I wish I could hate you
But the truth is I can't
Because every time I try
I think of the past

Of the good times we had
And even the bad
But mostly just the feelings we had

I loved you then
And I'll love you forever
Even if we never get back together

I wish you the best
Even if you hate me
I wish that someday
You could see some of these things

continued...

I would give you my last
And think nothing of it
I would give you the world
If I could afford it
Because you deserve it
Even if you don't know it
So you'll be in my heart
And on my mind

Because I'll always care for you
Until my end of time

DESOLATE ROAD

The road I travel
Is cold and white
With no one else around
Apparently not traveled much
With no footprints to be found

The road is somewhat desolate
And no signs to show the way
But somehow, I still forge on
And hope I'm going the right way

With darkness now my comfort
The only one I have
It no longer bothers me
That it envelops me fast

Now the trail has footprints
The ones that I have left
No longer just a desolate road
Plagued and full of death

LIES BELIEVED

With a promise of fortune
Comes an air of misfortune

Along with my truth
Stories riddled with lies
But for me, truth is constant
For my lies are not known

Trying my hardest
To make sure they're not shown
But is it really a lie
If no one knows it to be so?

Is it really not true
If only beknown to me
For now, my truths
I also believe
Now also believing
The things they believe

ENTITLED

As I look at those who came before
The battles that they fought
The battles to be seen as equals
And the liberties that they sought

I think of how so many now
Think so little of the past
So many opportunities squandered
Not thinking of building to last

So many seem to feel entitled
Instead of accomplished through blood and tears
Not realizing those who contributed to the struggle
Or the many lives lost over the years

The struggle so many try to ignore
With their large and infinite blinders
The struggle to which we are born
As the descendants of outsiders

continued...

Descendants of those thought of as lesser
By those seizing the opportunity to enslave
Taking advantage of a frightened people
And the naivety they portrayed
The frightened nature continues
As we continue to betray our own
Letting others instill a fear
For a community to which we belong

Until our past is realized
And we learn to work together
We will now and always remain
A powerful entity not yet energized

CALMER DAYS

Looking through the window
As the green looks book at me
Envious of the calm it shows
That I can no longer feel

The comfort of its breeze
Or its hot and muggy day
The songs of many birds
Chirping along the way

As they revel in its nature
With their childlike lack of care
No knowledge of the turmoil
Going on all around them

I wish for calmer days
To once again enjoy their beauty
As the world around me fades
Into the black abyss of confusion

continued…

Longing for the days of old
Getting lost within their beauty
Now just trying to remain safe
My only remaining duty
As the sun begins to fade
And the birds all fly away
The black replaces the green
As all that remains to be seen

HARVEST COLORS

Looking at the spots of white
Like an unrelenting sea
Scattered along the roadside
As far as the eye can see

The white mixed with the green
Of the husks of neighboring lines
The green towering above the white
With the slow passing of time

No longer showing brown of bolls
The white waits to be picked
Now becoming weighty bales
From many lines grown so thick

Now the green is tinged with brown
On the silk that it now colors
The clear liquid flowing down
A sign that it is ready

continued...

Ready to tower above no longer
But now be part of the harvest
Not far behind its white counterpart
On its still continuing journey
Making way for new browns and greens
With the coming of the next season
New plants to take over those grounds
Until it is once again their season

NIGHTLY SHOW

The gleaming from your brightest glow
For shows put on at night
Shows for anyone to enjoy
By looking up on a clear night

You are the calming illumination
That only night can bring
Performing with such dedication
Dawn bringing the end to your showing

Watching you when I want to get lost
In the beauty of your shine
Forgetting all my worldly fears
And losing track of time

For me, you've always been the calm
In this chaos considered life
The natural beauty put above
For everyone to admire

UNKNOWN WAR

Am I safe at home?
Or am I still in danger?
Did someone make a call?
Or does my home look like yours?

Getting a bowl of cereal
Like I did in my younger years
Should never lead to crime tape
Or my loved ones drowning in tears

In sitting on my own couch
And minding my own business
I was somehow still a threat
One that had to be negated

I stay out of your way
And yet this still is not enough
You go out of your way
To show that you are tough

You can destroy the lives of many
By moving just one finger
Taking the lives of so many
Seeming like your only remedy
Somehow you deserve to live
But I don't share that fate
Somehow you feel you were given the right
To determine another's fate

Maybe one day you will realize
That your hate won't get you far
In these otherwise uneventful days
That you have turned into a war

RESPECT

I have to teach my sons and daughters
To address you with respect
That the fear they feel is normal
With what has happened in retrospect

Don't make any sudden movements
Try not to look like a threat
Make sure your hands are always in view
Don't reach for anything

Speak with an air of intellect
For them and for yourself
Let them think you are worthy
Of a reciprocated respect

Try not to be in the wrong neighborhood
Or turn without using a signal
Try not to be in the wrong place
So you don't give them a reason

A reason for them to "fear" you
As an explanation of their use of force
A reason to make one more Black child
Be grieved by their mother
I want you to gain the respect
They failed to show to so many others
I want you to accomplish your dreams
Or at least die knowing that you outlived me

WAITING IN VAIN

What did I do to deserve this?
The pressure you apply to my neck
Applied with no consideration
Of my pain or lack of breath

I cried out for my mother
I cried out for myself
I cried out to a man
Who couldn't have cared less

To him, I was not human
Or, at least, so his actions said
Nothing more than a criminal
Who wouldn't amount to anything

He cared not for my children
Who would wait for me in vain
The father that, like so many,
Would not return again

No longer a part of their lives
Through no choices of my own
Now just a statistic
Instead of the man I strived to be
One that sparked a movement
To bring this hatred to its knees

Although this is just the start
I hope my death will bring some change
So no one else's children
Will have to sit and wait in vain

TRUE FORTITUDE

Today you took away my brother
Yesterday my best friend
Tomorrow will be my father
But when will be the end

Somehow you see within us
Something you don't like
Somehow when you look at us
All you feel is spite

Spite for what we stand for
Or what we have achieved
Spite for what we left behind
In the huts of slavery

You are no longer seen as masters
But more an equal to the slave
A testament to our forefathers
And the blood and lives they gave

Now we are the teachers
Instead of sneaking to learn to read
Because knowledge is power
And the only way to succeed
Once again, you fear our efforts
To rise up and be strong
To realize our true fortitude
And rise above it all

So you take away our black men
Into jails
Or in the ground
Hoping to deter the rest
From somehow breaking ground

But one day, you will realize
That the future is within the slave
Because we overcame it all
And became masters of our own fate

STILL THE MASTERS

The new form of slavery
Lies within a jail cell
Where they are still the masters
And we all must behave

Gaining beatings or solitude
For those that do misbehave
Now it's lights out
Now it's time to wake up
Now it's rec time
Now it's time to eat up

The routines may have changed
But the oppression remains the same
Now being given a number
Instead of identifying by a name

Just another way to strip humanity
From the already depressing setting
Just another way of showing
That they are still the masters

That they still hold the power
And we will always be seen as slaves
That until we know our true value
We will always misbehave

All they need is a reason
Which so many of us graciously give
That we don't deserve our freedom
And we don't deserve to live

Until we finally realize
We are the masters of ourselves
We will remain in the bondages of their system
Until our slow and meaningless deaths

HIDDEN HATRED

No longer easily identifiable
In your white and hooded attire
No longer using beatings and lynchings
Or destroying things by fire

Now you dress in business suits
Or issued uniforms
Now you have official reasons
To come into our homes

You come under the premise of one thing
With real intentions of another
You come with the façade of business
While really undercover

Because you have not changed
Your agenda or clear-cut biases
Because you refuse to abandon
Your unwarranted hatred for someone different

The times have changed your approach
But not your clearly perceived ending
Now I'm expected to carry on
With someone who lacks my best interest
What so many consider paranoia
Is now coming to the light
The struggle assigned at birth
With this longwinded color fight

Hoping as others for a generation
That will see past the faults of the past
And will gain a real solution
One that actually can last

That will put both sides on even ground
Not the nation divided we are
To accept and heal the many scars
And genuinely agree to move on

ONLY 12

All I was doing was playing
What else was I supposed to do
So I like to play with toy guns
As many others in their youth

It wasn't even mine
I got it from a friend
I would have let him keep it
Had I known how the story would end

He didn't give any warning
The car didn't even stop
I had no chance to tell my side
Before everything went wrong

I thought they were meant to help
Not take actions off assumptions
How is a 12-year-old kid
Deserving of this type of repercussion

I saw the incidents on the news
But never thought that this would be me
Some of those men were big and threatening
I haven't even reached my teens
I don't want to take away their lives
Though they thought so little about taking away mine
I just want them to take the time to think
Before just acting out

Not every situation
Requires the same use of force
Not every individual
Is out to get the law

Maybe just starting to consider
Before taking away someone's life
Maybe weighing other options
Instead of taking the most drastic route

REMINDERS

Never meant to hurt you
Or the one that you once bore
But it was the only true way
For me to ever hope to be whole

Although it was not your fault
You remind me of the pain
Take me back to old times
All those sad and miserable days

Days when I would go to sleep
With the biggest hope to not wake up
Days when I would look at people
Having nothing close to trust

Days when I would feel
That I was no longer me
Days when I couldn't even hold myself
Because of how much I hated me

I hated that I let myself ever be this weak
I hated that I wanted nothing more
than to just not be
I hated everything I saw
When I looked into the mirror
I hated that I looked at me
And saw nothing familiar

All my many hopes and dreams
Nothing more than memory
Memory fading with passing days
Along with the pieces of me

TORN WORLD

Letting go of memories
Of a pained and troubled past
Stuck with all the feelings and scars
That seem to forever last

I try to think of better times
But they seem so few and far between
I try to think of the love once had
For someone who was once my everything

All the clouds of darker times
Have swallowed up brighter days
All the rainbows once abound
Have now faded away

All that is seen is the storm you brought
When you trampled what was once a full heart
All that is remembered is the battles fought
When you tore my world apart

NIGHTMARES

The peace that I now feel
When at night I lay my head
Putting to rest the years of wanting
And wishing I were dead

Now there is this calm
That was once all turbulence
Now I can go home
And not worry about disturbance

Now they are just nightmares
Instead of dangerous and vivid truths
Nightmares I can wake from
No longer a continual loop

BLURRY PICTURE

Do they really understand
The words they read from me?
Do they really want to know
The picture that I see?

The picture that remains so dark
Without real shape or form
The picture that remains a blur
As I continue to look on

The blurry outlines of these pictures
Are what I strive to be,
Knowing no more of the destination
Than the little I can see

Is this even the right way
Or the me I was meant to be?
Will I ever really find out
What it means to just be me?

Maybe as I travel further
The picture will one day become clear
But since I have not seen that day
My heart still fills with fear

MISTAKEN STRENGTH

The picture is still not clearly seen
No matter the effort put forth
Even blurry in my dreams
Where everything was defined clearly before

How do I know where to go
Or what I am to do?
How do I know who to trust
Whose words actually ring true?

I let my guard down once before
And my heart still holds the scars
I tried before to love someone
Before I loved myself

Although I am still trying to find
The me that is worth love
I stumble across so many things
That were never brought to light
The struggles I fight within myself
Leading to my sleepless nights

continued…

I wonder if I will ever find
Someone that can love me
As I can't seem to find
Reason enough for me

I am this broken, shattered person
Who portrays this person of strength
Exhausted from the continued fighting
Of this war within myself

Hoping to one day lay down arms
And surrender to the thought
That somewhere somehow, I'm deserving of love
And be open to it like never before

NEVER MINE

Once again invading my thoughts
As you have always done
Once again, trying to convince me
That you were indeed that one

The one that I was meant to love
With whom I share my life
The one that I would love so much
And would want to make my wife

But even in invaded dreams
I remember the pain you caused
Even in my innermost thoughts
I can't forget what was lost

The way I used to look at you
Or get excited when you would call
The way that I would struggle with you
As we fought against them all

continued...

Now I know I fought alone
As you were never on my side
Your love was simply brushed away
Just like a passing tide
And now I know so many things
You tried so hard to hide

Why you still contain a place
In my head and in my heart
Is something I hope to figure out
And remove you from them both

DOUBTS

Why do I feel guilty
That I want you in my past?
Why does all the hurt and pain
Seem to always last?

I try my best not to think of you
But this never seems to work out
Maybe because deep inside
I still seem to have doubts

Doubts of whether feelings were true
Or am I making wrong decisions
Doubts of who I thought you to be
In my deepest darkest visions

Forever you seem to have a hold
On my heart as well as my mind
The more I try to break the hold
The more it seems to bind

continued…

Things that were supposed to bind
I thought were all erased
Leaving behind only memories
And I thought very little trace
But now I wonder if the guilt I feel
Is for wanting to find another to love
When you were supposed to be that one

I think I may have convinced myself
That you were more than you really were
And now I truly seek the one
For whom my soul will lay bare

DELUSIONAL LOVE

When I sit back and wonder where it all went wrong
I always come to the same conclusion
I always loved you
But your love was just an illusion

Something that I wanted to see
So I made myself see it
Something that I wanted to feel
So I made myself feel it

In your eyes, I always saw the truth
That you were never mine to have
Your actions always showed the truth
That you were on a different path

A path that didn't include me
Or the life I wanted for the future
A path that only you could lead
With some other person featured

continued...

I kept it going for so long
In my head and in my heart
But you would never play the part
Which forced me to move on
Looking for that true love
That I tried to force with you
That love that could look into my eyes
And I could truly see it

No longer looking for that solace
As in your arms, I'll feel it
In your arms, I'll feel the truth
That only you can show
In your arms, I'll feel the love
That only we can know

With every long and passing day
I wait for your embrace
Knowing it will prove worth the wait
To bask in your embrace

PROMISE

A sigh of relief
And hope for the future
Swept all over me
That 7th day of November

The feeling of promise
The day now provided
No longer feeling dread
At a divided nation, undecided

Wondering if healing could now set in
Or is it just a prelude for the hatred once again

MY APOLOGY

I feel the weight lift off my mind
As the memories fade away
No longer just looking to find
A way to pass the days

Now I try to live my life
Not thinking of living for you
I wonder how I spent so much time
Crippling myself with your pain

Trying so hard to gain your love
Trying so hard in vain
Now I try to love myself
Something I've been avoiding for years

The peace I never knew it brings
Now bringing me to tears
No longer tears of fear and pain
But tears of utter joy

Feeling I finally made it through
An utterly elusive door
As I shut behind me the darkness of past
And what I used to be
I fall to my knees and thank the one
That helped me to get free

Free of all the pain I caused
To others and to myself
As I waded through the darkness
In my unforgiving past

I apologize for the selfish acts
I used to try to survive
I apologize for not seeing the truth
That I was convincing myself of the lies

I am now in a better place
In life and in myself
And hope to influence others
Not to follow my dark path

TRUST

Do I trust the help they give?
Or is it impure motives?
Can I trust the serum provided?
Or was it meant to end us?

Those of us not strong enough
To weather this hard fight
Those of us foolish enough
To trust what you're doing is right

The paranoia now setting in
From years of failed coexistence
Now I am meant to blindly trust
The vial that you are giving

Is my vial the same as yours
Or is it a lesser solution?
Am I just an unknowing volunteer
In a trial meant to better your living?

Is it really worth the risk
And a strive back toward normal?
Or is it just another way
To portray the façade of normal?

THE NATION I LOVE

As I kneel on the ground
The same is done to my rights
Constantly demanding me to rise
Why can't they do the same

Rise past the oppression they so openly give
Come to the understanding
that everyone deserves to live

You accuse me of betrayal of the country I love
Though I've already served my time
Unlike many making these declarations
That I don't respect my country
Or fellow brothers and sisters that protect it

That my current beliefs
Are nothing more than cries for attention
Attention that we would not need to receive
If everything were equal as it was supposed to be

continued...

I would have given my life if it was required
As was the agreement that late October

But now I am treated
Like the enemy I was trained to fight
Like an enemy of the nation
Or a thief in the night

I continue to love my country
Though it seems to hate me
As it cuts off my airway
And I struggle to breathe

I will give my last breath
If it brings understanding
That true and equal rights
Are worth the demanding

REAL LOVE

The love I seem to find within
With every passing day
A love I never felt with you
In the same type of way

A love where I could be myself
And never have to fear
A love where simple misunderstandings
Would not end with tears

Tears for what I thought I had
In a person thought to be my dream
Tears of one lost long ago
One that was once me

I now look forward to the coming days
Instead of feelings of dread
No longer overwhelming feelings of hatred
Clouding up my head

continued…

I hated what I had become
And so many things I had done
Hated who I turned into
Trying to impress someone
Now I know you weren't my one
And I could actually be enough
When I finally find the person
I can really truly trust

I love that I now feel some hope
No longer just guilt and pain
I hope that with enough time
Love will be all that remains

FUTURE WIFE

Getting lost in those dreamy brown eyes
That draw me into your soul
The curls that caress my fingers
With their brown and silky hold

The radiance of your skin
Reflecting the brightness within
The colors dancing across your body
Reflecting places you have been

The lovers from your past
Or the pain that still remains
The fading scars they left behind
With their never-ending games

As I run my hands across them
The lines that bare your soul
I feel the very essence of you
As it makes my heart whole

continued…

Hearing your voice as melodies
Singing the story of our life
Holding on to every word
Of my beautiful future wife
Everything about you
Reflects perfection in human form
Being reminded every day
While together we grow old

THE RIVER

Below the murky surface
Near your littered bumpy streets
There flows a type of peacefulness
For everyone to see

You remind me of my playful youth
Summers spent playing near your banks
Remind me of the true serenity
This type of place can bring

Looking at you reminds me
Of the city I love so much
Where I look at you with admiration
While most just looked with disgust

To them, you were a dirty reminder
Of nature lost to human contamination
To me, you were and will always remain
A beautiful reminder of summer living

RAW EMOTIONS

Today you had to make a choice
That reminded me of mine
The day filled with so much pain
I felt that it stopped time

I had to let go of someone
Who never let go of me
I had to let go of my heart
While trying to remember to breathe

The person who always exuded love
For everyone she met
The one who rarely had her own
From helping everyone else get

I'm sorry I couldn't be with you
As you exited this life
Overcome with raw emotions
The main one being strife

You left me in this awful world
In which I never belonged
Left me to fight my many battles
I put off for so long
I hope you can forgive me
For the person I became
No longer the one you gave life to
Just masquerading around with her name

JUDGMENT

Why should I be judged
For the person that I choose?
Not like you have a stake
Or something that you will lose

My choices are my own
As are yours to you
But somehow, my choice makes you uneasy
Like yours are oh so true

Unlike most of you
I care not who you choose
As you will be the only one
That your choice will need to prove

I avoid the continual judgment
That you seem so eager to give
Like someone asked for your advice
On the life that I should live

I will continue to subdue my opinions
Which should be a subtle hint
That you should do the same
And to the same extent

HIDDEN EMPTINESS

The meaningless caress
That was placed upon your face
Like so many others
In this never-ending race

I reached for you from loneliness
I reached for you from fear
As I did with many others
In the quickly passing years

I reached out for connection
That for once would not be her
I reached out for a lover
That she finally would not deter

I reached out for my other half
But was left emptier than before
I gave what I could to please them
But in the end, they wanted more

continued…

They wanted access to my heart
As broken as it was
They wanted a true openness
But there was, of course, one clause
I lost sight of many feelings
Through losses over the years
And have reached a sort of conclusion
In spite of all my fears

I was not meant to love the ones
That have real love for me
But to forever pine over the ones
That bring me to my knees

The ones that care not of feelings
Or the hurt they seem to bring
The ones that know of nothing more
But to live in and inflict pain

I come back to the pain I have
And even the pain I've caused
And know that this is meant to be
For me, above it all

DESCENDING DARKNESS

Trying to escape the thoughts
Continually clouding my head
Knowing that I'm not enough
And I would be better off dead

Every day I continue this façade
That I am okay with who I am
The darkness again descends
While I try not to let it in

As it waits for no invitation
To infiltrate my melancholy space
It takes over my soul
With the simplest of haste

FORGOTTEN FACE

Almost like you feel me happy
Or just moved on from you
Call me with your negativity
After all you put me through

You don't deserve to have a thought
Or opinions about what I do
Like you weren't the main reason
I wanted my life through

You brought with you a darker side
That many like you have
Brought deep from within me
A side I've tried to hide

You let me see the person buried
So far back in my past
Let me see a side of me
I'd forgotten that I had

But somehow, you looked deep inside
And saw a familiar face
Saw the part of me left behind
After so much I loved passed away
But for me, you will always be the one
That only cares for self
You will always put your wants
Above everyone else

The selfish being you have become
Is who I've avoided in myself
The person in my mirror long ago
That only cared for self

TRUE ENEMY

Once again, invading my space
Along with my sanity
Not that you ever cared
About trampling either thing

Now I can look back and see
All the pain you caused
Now I can truly see
That you really care for no one

So much time you spent reminding me
Of feelings you claimed to have
So much time spent convincing me
Of enemies in my past

Now I can see the true enemy
Was in the form of you
Someone who pretended to care
For me and those I loved

Someone trying to be there for me
When I laid my mother to rest
But much unknown to you
I made a promise I will never forget
That I will never again fall for your lies
Or your made-up regrets

You were the one that tried to break
The person I tried to be
But when she took her last breath
I forcefully set you free

WILL TO LIVE

A letter to myself
Who so stupidly went rushing in
Into a complicated situation
Just for the experience

Saying if I could change one thing
That would definitely be you
Would be the biggest understatement
That could ever ring true

I wish that you never graced anyone
With what you consider presence
I wish that I never heard your name
Or learned of your existence

I often wish I never was
Now I wish that for us both
No longer able to hurt the ones
That have loved us the most

Most of those that have loved me
Have left me over the years
And all I could do is sit and wait
To like them walk away
Walk away from the very existence
That has plagued me over the years
The life that only kept me here
Because of a mother's tears

But now that I have no mother left
I have no reason to live
I spend my days muddling through
With nothing else to give

When I let her go in that October
I let go of the rest of me
Knowing that what left with her
Was my remaining will to live

STATE OF LIFE

Now that I let my guard down
And actually want to try
Now becomes the time
That all choose to now fly

Fly away from commitment
Fly away from reality
Flying toward a goal
Seen as an abnormality

Why are things so different now
Than the last time that I tried
Why do I seem so out of touch
With the current state of life

I wish that I had found love then
When I didn't care to try
Wish that I had found myself
Instead of accepting a lie

WITHOUT RESPONSE

So much time spent waiting
For a response that never comes
In my head, debating,
How I keep choosing these ones

The ones that seem to reel me in
Then hang me out to dry
The ones that show much interest
Then disappear without a why

Why they don't seem to like me
Why I'm not worth their attention
Why they can't seem to be honest
And admit no wanted retention

I'm not as fragile as they seem to think
I have heard rejection before
At least I wouldn't keep coming back
Disillusioned that there is more

continued...

More than just a passing hello
Or exchange of pictures and thoughts
The building of something serious
Something from the heart
But continuing to sit without response
To the simplest of exchanges
Only solidifying in my mind
The desperately needed changes

Maybe I need to change my type
The woman that catches my eye
Or just lower my expectations
To the opposite of high

Maybe I should just exit this ring
That seems so full of loss
And move onto different focuses
Where I can be the boss

MIRRORED PASTS

Waking up with the utmost joy
Expecting a text from you
Bringing a smile to my morning
Like only you can do

My dreams are filled with thoughts of you
And things that we will do
My imagination running wild
Like it has a tendency to do

I think of all the many places
We will visit in our life
Think of all the days we'll share
After you become my wife

It seemed this day would never come
And I would never find true love
But you have now appeared
Like the perfect gift from above

continued…

Our stories seemed like mirrored pasts
As we take the time to share
Wanting the same in the future
And sharing the same fears
Taking only moments to miss you
When our time is spent apart
I know how much you mean to me
And that you share my heart

YOUR SUNLIGHT

All the darkness gone away
From rays of your sunlight
Bringing brightness to my day
And a newfound delight

You became my sunshine
When all I knew was dark
Replacing all the emptiness
And rebuilding my heart

I know that I will care for you
Until my dying day
Because you helped me see the truth
Making colors out of gray

MY MERMAID

I think I'm starting to love you
But is it just too soon
How can I stop these feelings
From developing so soon

From the day I saw you
I knew who you could be
My forever Ariel
Or my mermaid in the sea

Always below the surface
So you were not seen before
But I managed to see a glimpse of you
And knew I wanted more

I wanted to be your Eric
Or your Erica, to be exact
I wanted to be your everything
And have everything they lacked

Every night I think of you
Swimming alone in the sea
But even in my dreams
You seem just beyond my reach
Are you just a fairytale
Like the cartoon from my youth
Or are you the real thing
And your words are just the truth

I lose my heart to your gentle song
Humming through the night
I lose my heart to your words
That I believe with all my might

I hang on to your promises
And hope that they stay true
Because you are my Ariel
And you, I will not lose

www.ingramcontent.com/pod-product-compliance
Lightning Source LLC
Chambersburg PA
CBHW050656160426
43194CB00010B/1963